Marks and Spencer p.l.c.
Baker Street, London, W1U 8EP

www.marksandspencer.com

All titles in the series subject to availability

ISBN: 1-84273-915-8

Printed in China

Produced by the Bridgewater Book Company Ltd.

Photographer Calvey Taylor-Haw

Home Economist Ruth Pollock

NOTES FOR THE READER

- This book uses both metric and imperial measurements. Follow the same units of measurement throughout; do not mix metric and imperial.
- All spoon measurements are level: teaspoons are assumed to be 5 ml, and tablespoons are assumed to be 15 ml.
- Unless otherwise stated, milk is assumed to be full fat, eggs and individual vegetables such as potatoes are medium and pepper is freshly ground black pepper.
- Recipes using raw or very lightly cooked eggs should be avoided by infants, the elderly, pregnant women, convalescents and anyone suffering from an illness.
- The times given are an approximate guide only. Preparation times differ according to the techniques used by different people and the cooking times may also vary from those given. Optional ingredients, variations or serving suggestions have not been included in the calculations.

contents

introduction

Organic produce can maximize the health benefits of a diet rich in vegetables, fruit and oily fish.

Nowadays, we are becoming much more conscious of the food we eat and how it is produced. 'You are what you eat' has become a familiar phrase, and given that there is a direct relationship between what we eat and the state of our health, it is clear that a safe, healthy diet is a very important part of our wellbeing.

Yet the choices we have to make can be overwhelming. Never before has such a wide variety of foods been available. How do we choose the most healthy foods? How can we ensure that they are safe?

Advances in science have brought many welcome benefits in terms of food supply and our increased understanding of nutrition. With these advances, however, have come increasing concerns about modern methods of food production. Food scares have become a regular feature in the media. We often read about outbreaks of food poisoning and the dangers of pesticides. Now we are also having to consider genetically modified (GM) foods. While some experts are hailing these as the new way to ensure pest-resistant foods, others are concerned about the techniques being used and their long-term effects on our health.

Even if we disregard fears about GM foods, the use of synthetic fertilizers, chemical pesticides and food additives raises concerns for the consumer. In addition, some food additives have been linked with health problems such as asthma and heart disease. They have also been associated with unwanted conditions such as allergic reactions, hyperactivity, nausea, palpitations and mood swings. No wonder people are turning to organic food as a healthy and safe alternative.

Organic fruit is grown without potentially harmful chemicals.

So what exactly is organic food? There is a popular misconception that it is something for healthfood fanatics and not for ordinary food-lovers, but this is not true. An organic meal could, for example, consist of a succulent rump steak accompanied by white bread and a bottle of full-bodied red wine. This might be followed by an indulgent chocolate-and-cream dessert. Children can enjoy a dinner of beefburgers, chips and tomato ketchup, made completely from organic ingredients.

Organic food is simply food that has been produced in a farming system that seeks to avoid the use of artificial chemicals, pesticides and other additives. This does not mean that it cannot be exciting. In this book you might be surprised to find recipes ranging from roasts to pizzas, and from puddings to meringues. As you will see, organic cooking can produce meals that are just as enticing as ordinary cooking.

Organic varieties of many different kinds of bread are now widely available.

Organic farmers produce their foods by developing a healthy, fertile soil. They avoid using weedkillers, preferring instead to control weeds by mechanical cultivation techniques and by hand. Instead of using artificial pesticides, organic farmers use nature's way of controlling pests. They introduce insects that kill the pests but do not harm the crops. They plant and protect trees and hedges, to provide habitats for natural predators such as beetles and spiders which in turn help to keep down pests. Organic farmers also rear animals in a more humane way, without feeding them cocktails of drugs, hormones and antibiotics. Animals are kept in natural, free-range conditions and fed a more natural diet, ensuring they are healthy and can move around freely. The end result is natural, healthier produce.

Sales of organic food and drink have increased rapidly in the UK and the trend is set to continue.

Organic farming is also kinder to the environment. It encourages a wider diversity of plants and wildlife such as birds and butterflies, and nurtures the soil. The Soil Association, an organization which promotes organic food and farming, says that it takes at least two years for a farm to become organic, and often much longer. This is because it takes time for the land to recover and for artificial chemical levels to be reduced. Organic farming helps restore a natural balance to exhausted soil, and increases its fertility.

GM technology is banned in organic farming, even in organic animal feed. Every possible care is taken to avoid cross-pollination in order to ensure that organic crops are not contaminated by GM crops in neighbouring fields. In this way, you can be sure that the food you eat has grown in the way that nature intended.

Organic food is becoming more and more popular, with food and drink sales in the UK now totalling around £1 billion each year. Around 20% of fresh fruit and vegetables sold in supermarkets is organic, and two-thirds of baby food is organic. Organic restaurants are also on the increase. Living the organic way does not have to mean simply eating organic food, however. It can also become a way of life. You can now buy a whole host of organic products, such as clothing, cosmetics and gardening products.

To keep fruits and vegetables natural, GM technology is banned from organic farming.

The term 'organic' is defined by law, and the industry is highly regulated in the UK. Suppliers must abide by strict rules in order for their products to be accepted as organic. There are a number of certification bodies in the UK, of which the Soil Association is the most widely known. When you are buying organic products, look for the Soil Association symbol, the Marks and Spencer 'O' symbol, or labelling from other reputable bodies, as guarantees of the highest organic standards.

In most supermarkets you will find a wide range of organic foods. In addition to fresh fruit and vegetables, meat, poultry, dairy products, and white and wholemeal bread, you will find convenient fast foods, prepared meals, crisps, biscuits, snacks, chocolate bars, soups, sauces, beers, ciders, wines and a good selection of frozen foods. When you buy fish, remember that in the UK fish caught in the wild cannot be sold as organic. However, you can buy organic fish that have been reared in fish farms. Many supermarkets now stock organic farmed fish, such as trout and salmon. Some organic shellfish, such as mussels, are also becoming available, but you may need to buy them from a specialist supplier.

Food marked with the Marks and Spencer 'O' symbol has been produced organically, to strict environmental and animal welfare standards.

coffee & walnut cake page 88

Within the pages of this book you will find recipes to tempt all kinds of tastes, whether you are cooking for meat-eaters or vegetarians. All of the recipes use ingredients of which there are organic varieties widely available in supermarkets.

Why not try the Cheese & Ham Pizzas (page 46) or the Salmon Steaks with Lime Salsa (page 64)? Or how about the Mushroom Risotto (page 60), Maple Roast Lamb with Cider (page 70) or Stuffed Roast Pork with Garlic (page 72)? For dessert, the Chocolate Cups (page 94) are irresistible, and a slice of Coffee & Walnut Cake (page 88) with a cup of freshly brewed organic coffee is a must. So, whether you are planning a dinner party, cooking an everyday family meal, or preparing a quick and simple snack for yourself, there is bound to be an organic recipe in this book to suit the occasion.

guide to recipe key		
	very easy	Recipes are graded as follows: 1 pea = easy; 2 peas = very easy; 3 peas = extremely easy.
	serves 4	Recipes generally serve four people. Simply halve the ingredients to serve two, taking care not to mix metric and imperial measurements.
	10 minutes	Preparation time. Where marinating or soaking are involved, these times have been added on separately: e.g. 15 minutes + 30 minutes to marinate.
	10 minutes	Cooking time. Cooking times do not include the cooking of side dishes or accompaniments served with the main dishes.

country chicken broth
page 16

stuffed tomatoes
page 50

mushroom risotto
page 60

peach & strawberry meringue
page 92

soups, starters & salads

There are some real treats in store for cooks and food lovers in the following pages. Many of the starters can double up as snacks or as satisfying meals in themselves. Add some fresh crusty bread to the Herbed Potato & Cheddar Soup, for example, or the Country Chicken Broth, and you will find they make substantial lunches. The Stuffed Red Peppers with Basil, and the Chicken & Mixed Herb Pâté are full of fresh flavour, while the salad recipes featured here are vibrant with colour and texture. They make great accompaniments, starters or light meals.

mixed bean & herb soup

very easy	
serves 4	
20 minutes + 8 hours to soak	
1 hour 55 minutes	

ingredients

- 125 g/4½ oz dried chickpeas
- 125 g/4½ oz dried black-eyed beans
- 1 tbsp vegetable oil
- 1 garlic clove, chopped
- 2 spring onions, sliced
- 2 leeks, chopped
- 1 potato, chopped
- 1 carrot, chopped
- 1 bay leaf
- 1 tbsp chopped fresh thyme
- 1.2 litres/2 pints vegetable stock
- 600 ml/1 pint water
- salt and pepper
- 1 tbsp snipped fresh chives, plus extra for garnishing
- 1 tbsp chopped fresh parsley

fresh crusty bread, to serve

Rinse and drain the chickpeas and black-eyed beans, put them into a bowl, then cover generously with cold water and leave to soak for at least 8 hours or overnight. Drain the beans, put them into a saucepan and add enough cold water to cover the beans by about 5 cm/2 inches. Bring to the boil, then boil the beans rapidly for 10 minutes. Drain, rinse well, then drain again and set aside.

Heat the oil in a large saucepan over a medium–low heat. Add the garlic, spring onions and leeks and cook, stirring, for 3 minutes until slightly softened. Add the potato and carrot and cook for a further 2 minutes, then add the beans, bay leaf, thyme, stock and water. Season to taste with salt and pepper. Bring to the boil, then reduce the heat, cover the pan and simmer, stirring occasionally, for 1½ hours, or until the beans are tender. Remove and discard the bay leaf. Stir in the chives and the chopped parsley, ladle into bowls and garnish with chives. Serve with fresh crusty bread.

herbed potato & cheddar soup

very easy	
serves 4	
20 minutes	
40 minutes	

ingredients

- 1½ tbsp vegetable oil
- 1 garlic clove, chopped
- 1 large onion, chopped
- 2 medium potatoes, chopped
- 1 large carrot, chopped
- 1 bay leaf
- 600 ml/1 pint vegetable stock
- salt and pepper
- 25 g/1 oz butter, softened
- 2 tbsp chopped fresh parsley
- 2 tbsp snipped fresh chives
- 100–115 g/3½–4 oz fresh crusty bread, lightly toasted
- 90 g/3¼ oz Cheddar cheese, coarsely grated

Heat the oil in a large saucepan over a medium–low heat. Add the garlic and onion and cook, stirring, for 4 minutes until slightly softened. Add the potatoes and carrot and cook, stirring, for a further 5 minutes. Add the bay leaf and stock and season to taste with salt and pepper. Bring to the boil, then reduce the heat, cover the pan and simmer, stirring occasionally, for 25 minutes, or until the vegetables are tender.

Meanwhile, put the butter into a small bowl and beat in half the parsley and half the chives. Spread on to the toasted bread and top with the cheese. Cut into small chunks about 2.5-cm/1-inch square and set aside. Remove and discard the bay leaf from the soup.

Leave the soup to cool slightly, then transfer to a food processor and process for 1 minute, or until smooth. Return to a large, clean saucepan, stir in the remaining herbs and re-heat gently. Ladle into bowls, divide the chunks of bread between the bowls and serve.

country chicken broth

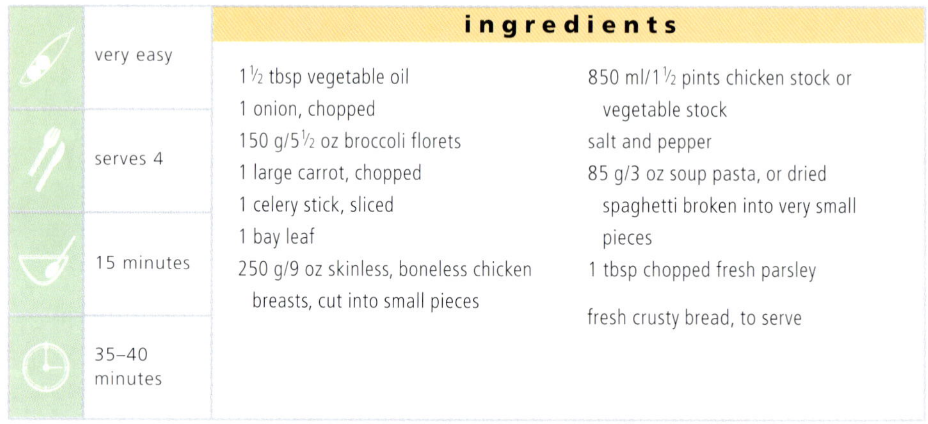

very easy

serves 4

15 minutes

35–40 minutes

ingredients

- 1½ tbsp vegetable oil
- 1 onion, chopped
- 150 g/5½ oz broccoli florets
- 1 large carrot, chopped
- 1 celery stick, sliced
- 1 bay leaf
- 250 g/9 oz skinless, boneless chicken breasts, cut into small pieces
- 850 ml/1½ pints chicken stock or vegetable stock
- salt and pepper
- 85 g/3 oz soup pasta, or dried spaghetti broken into very small pieces
- 1 tbsp chopped fresh parsley

fresh crusty bread, to serve

Heat the vegetable oil in a large saucepan over a medium–low heat. Add the onion and cook, stirring, for 4 minutes, or until slightly softened. Add the broccoli, carrot and celery and cook, stirring, for a further 4 minutes.

Add the bay leaf, chicken, stock, and salt and pepper to taste. Bring to the boil, then reduce the heat, cover the pan and simmer, stirring occasionally, for 10 minutes. Stir in the pasta, return to the boil and cook for a further 12 minutes until tender.

Remove and discard the bay leaf. Stir in the parsley, ladle into bowls and serve with fresh crusty bread.

ham & lentil soup

very easy	
serves 4	
20 minutes + 2 hours to soak	
1½ hours	

ingredients

225 g/8 oz red split lentils
1.5 litres/2¾ pints vegetable stock
1 garlic clove, chopped
1 onion, chopped
1 leek, chopped
1 large carrot, chopped
5 tomatoes, peeled and chopped
1 bay leaf
salt and pepper
175 g/6 oz potatoes, chopped
75 g/2¾ oz sweet potato, chopped
150 g/5½ oz smoked ham, diced
pinch of ground nutmeg

TO GARNISH
4 tbsp soured cream
paprika

fresh crusty bread, to serve

Put the lentils into a large saucepan, pour in the stock and leave to soak for 2 hours. Add the garlic, onion, leek, carrot, tomatoes and bay leaf, and season to taste with salt and pepper. Bring to the boil, then reduce the heat, cover the pan and simmer for 1 hour, stirring occasionally.

Add all the potatoes with the ham, cover the pan again and simmer for a further 25 minutes, or until the potatoes are tender.

Remove and discard the bay leaf. Transfer half the soup to a food processor and process for 1 minute, or until smooth. Return the mixture to the saucepan containing the rest of the soup, add the nutmeg and adjust the seasoning to taste, then re-heat gently until warmed through. Ladle into bowls, garnish with a spoonful of soured cream and sprinkle over a little paprika. Serve with fresh crusty bread.

stuffed red peppers with basil

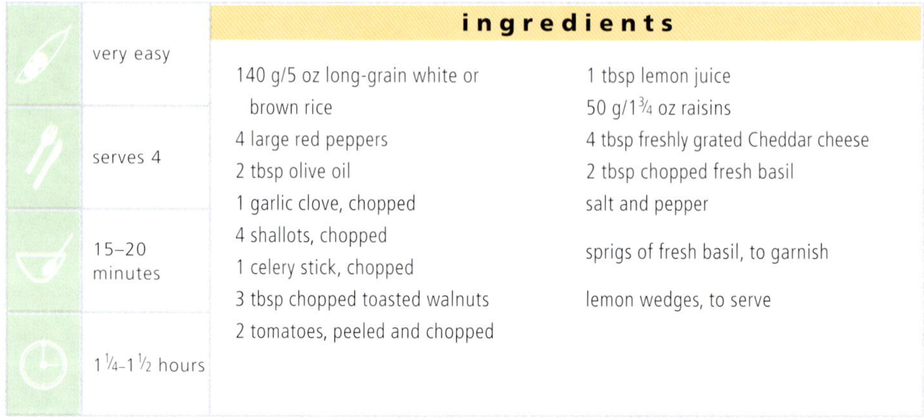

very easy

serves 4

15–20 minutes

1¼–1½ hours

ingredients

- 140 g/5 oz long-grain white or brown rice
- 4 large red peppers
- 2 tbsp olive oil
- 1 garlic clove, chopped
- 4 shallots, chopped
- 1 celery stick, chopped
- 3 tbsp chopped toasted walnuts
- 2 tomatoes, peeled and chopped
- 1 tbsp lemon juice
- 50 g/1¾ oz raisins
- 4 tbsp freshly grated Cheddar cheese
- 2 tbsp chopped fresh basil
- salt and pepper

- sprigs of fresh basil, to garnish

- lemon wedges, to serve

Cook the rice in a saucepan of lightly salted boiling water for 20 minutes if using white rice, or 35 minutes if using brown. Drain, rinse under cold running water, then drain again.

Using a sharp knife, cut the tops off the peppers and reserve. Remove the seeds and white cores, then blanch the peppers and reserved tops in boiling water for 2 minutes. Remove from the heat and drain well. Heat half the oil in a large frying pan, add the garlic and shallots and cook, stirring, for 3 minutes. Add the celery, walnuts, tomatoes, lemon juice and raisins and cook for a further 5 minutes. Remove from the heat and stir in the cheese, chopped basil and seasoning.

Preheat the oven to 180°C/350°F/Gas Mark 4. Stuff the peppers with the rice mixture and arrange them in a baking dish. Put the tops on the peppers, drizzle over the remaining oil, loosely cover with foil and bake in the preheated oven for 45 minutes. Remove from the oven. Garnish with basil sprigs and serve with lemon wedges.

chicken & mixed herb pâté

extremely easy	
serves 4	
15 minutes + 45 minutes to chill	
10 minutes	

ingredients

1 small floury potato, diced
250 g/9 oz cooked skinless chicken meat, diced
1 garlic clove, crushed
1 tbsp chopped fresh parsley
1 tbsp chopped fresh coriander
½ tbsp grated lemon rind
2 tbsp lemon juice
salt and pepper
100 g/3½ oz cream cheese
sliced spring onion, to garnish

TO SERVE
pitta bread, cut into triangles
vegetable crudités, such as carrots and celery
lemon wedges

Cook the diced potato in a saucepan of boiling water for 10 minutes, or until tender, then drain well.

Transfer the potato to a food processor, then add the chicken, garlic, parsley, coriander, lemon rind and juice, and salt and pepper to taste. Process until thoroughly blended. Alternatively, finely chop all the ingredients and mix together well.

Put the mixture into a large bowl and stir in the cream cheese. Cover with clingfilm and refrigerate for 45 minutes.

Remove from the refrigerator and divide the pâté between individual serving dishes. Sprinkle over the sliced spring onion to garnish and serve with pitta bread triangles, vegetable crudités and lemon wedges.

avocado salad with lime dressing

extremely easy

serves 4

20 minutes

—

ingredients

60 g/2¼ oz mixed fresh red and green lettuce leaves
60 g/2¼ oz fresh wild rocket
4 spring onions, finely diced
5 tomatoes, sliced
25 g/1 oz walnuts, toasted and chopped
2 avocados
1 tbsp lemon juice

LIME DRESSING
1 tbsp lime juice
1 tsp French mustard
1 tbsp crème fraîche
1 tbsp chopped fresh parsley or coriander
3 tbsp extra-virgin olive oil
pinch of sugar
salt and pepper

Wash and drain the lettuce and rocket, if necessary. Shred all the leaves and arrange in the bottom of a large salad bowl. Add the spring onions, tomatoes and walnuts.

Halve, peel and stone the avocados and cut into thin slices or small chunks. Brush with the lemon juice to prevent discolouration, then transfer to the salad bowl. Mix together gently.

Put the dressing ingredients into a screw-top jar, screw on the lid tightly and shake well until thoroughly combined. Drizzle the dressing over the salad and serve immediately.

feta cheese salad

extremely easy	
serves 4	
20 minutes	
—	

ingredients

50 g/1¾ oz fresh green salad leaves
handful of fresh coriander leaves
½ cucumber, chopped
4 spring onions, finely diced
4 tomatoes, sliced
12 black olives, stoned and sliced
140 g/5 oz feta cheese (if organic feta cheese is unavailable, use organic goat's cheese or mozzarella cheese instead)

CORIANDER DRESSING
4 tbsp extra-virgin olive oil
1 tbsp lime juice
1 tbsp chopped fresh coriander
salt and pepper

Wash and drain the salad leaves, if necessary. Shred the leaves and arrange in the bottom of a large salad bowl. Add the coriander leaves, cucumber, spring onions, tomatoes and olives.

Cut the cheese into thin slices or small chunks, then transfer to the salad bowl. Mix together gently.

Put the dressing ingredients into a screw-top jar, screw on the lid tightly and shake well until thoroughly combined. Drizzle the dressing over the salad and serve immediately.

smoked salmon & wild rocket salad

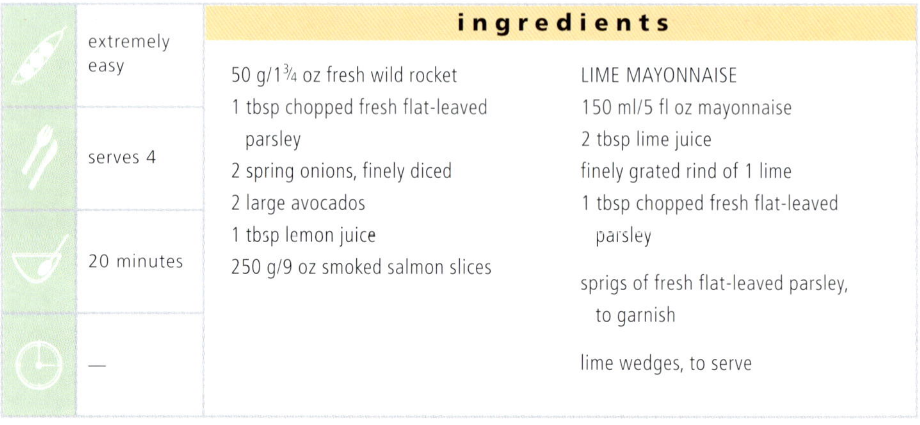

extremely easy

serves 4

20 minutes

—

ingredients

50 g/1¾ oz fresh wild rocket
1 tbsp chopped fresh flat-leaved parsley
2 spring onions, finely diced
2 large avocados
1 tbsp lemon juice
250 g/9 oz smoked salmon slices

LIME MAYONNAISE
150 ml/5 fl oz mayonnaise
2 tbsp lime juice
finely grated rind of 1 lime
1 tbsp chopped fresh flat-leaved parsley

sprigs of fresh flat-leaved parsley, to garnish

lime wedges, to serve

Wash and drain the rocket, if necessary. Shred the leaves and arrange in 4 individual salad bowls or on 4 small plates. Top with the chopped parsley and spring onions.

Halve, peel and stone the avocados and cut into thin slices or small chunks. Brush with the lemon juice to prevent discolouration, then divide between the salad bowls. Mix together gently. Cut the smoked salmon into strips and scatter over the top.

Put the mayonnaise into a bowl, then add the lime juice and rind and the chopped parsley. Mix together well. Spoon some of the lime mayonnaise on top of each salad, garnish with parsley sprigs and serve with lime wedges.

roast chicken salad with orange dressing

extremely easy	
serves 4	
20 minutes	
—	

ingredients

250 g/9 oz young spinach leaves
handful of fresh parsley leaves
½ cucumber, thinly sliced
90 g/3¼ oz walnuts, toasted and chopped
350 g/12 oz boneless lean roast chicken, thinly sliced
2 red apples
1 tbsp lemon juice

ORANGE DRESSING
2 tbsp extra-virgin olive oil
juice of 1 orange
finely grated rind of ½ orange
1 tbsp crème fraîche

sprigs of fresh flat-leaved parsley, to garnish

orange wedges, to serve

Wash and drain the spinach and parsley leaves, if necessary, then arrange on a large serving platter. Top with the cucumber and walnuts. Arrange the chicken slices over the salad.

Core the apples, then cut them in half. Cut each half into slices and brush with the lemon juice to prevent discolouration. Arrange the apple slices on top of the salad.

Put the dressing ingredients into a screw-top jar, screw on the lid tightly and shake well until thoroughly combined. Drizzle the dressing over the salad, garnish with parsley sprigs and serve with orange wedges.

light meals & side dishes

The light meals in this section are deliciously satisfying, yet simple to make. The Cheese & Vegetable Pasties are delicious at any time of day, and excellent for picnics and lunchboxes. The succulent Salmon Morsels are quick and easy to prepare – ideal for those days when time is short – and the Red Onion Tartlets and Fragrant Chicken Parcels will have everyone clamouring for more. This chapter also features tempting side dishes, such as Steamed Vegetables en Papillotes and Classic Roast Potatoes, which make perfect accompaniments for a wide range of main courses.

jacket potatoes with cream & walnuts

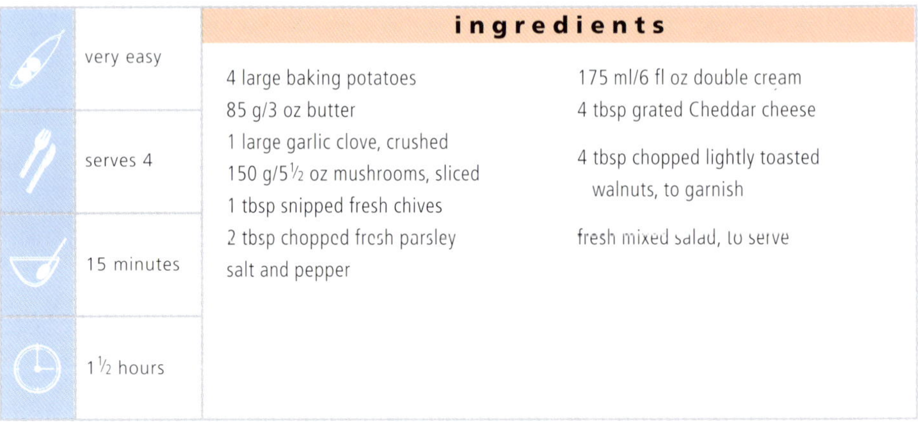

very easy

serves 4

15 minutes

1½ hours

ingredients

- 4 large baking potatoes
- 85 g/3 oz butter
- 1 large garlic clove, crushed
- 150 g/5½ oz mushrooms, sliced
- 1 tbsp snipped fresh chives
- 2 tbsp chopped fresh parsley
- salt and pepper
- 175 ml/6 fl oz double cream
- 4 tbsp grated Cheddar cheese

- 4 tbsp chopped lightly toasted walnuts, to garnish

- fresh mixed salad, to serve

Preheat the oven to 190°C/375°F/Gas Mark 5. Scrub the potatoes and pierce the skins several times with a fork. Place on a baking tray and cook in the preheated oven for 1¼ hours, or until cooked through. About 5 minutes before the end of the cooking time, melt 1½ tablespoons of the butter in a frying pan over a low heat, add the garlic and mushrooms and cook, stirring, for 4 minutes, or until the mushrooms are tender. Remove from the heat and set aside.

Remove the potatoes from the oven and cut them in half lengthways. Carefully scoop out the potato flesh into a bowl, leaving the skins intact. Add the remaining butter to the potato flesh, then stir in the herbs. Season to taste with salt and pepper. Spoon the mixture into the potato skins, then add a layer of mushrooms. Top with the cream, then the cheese.Return the potatoes to the oven and bake for another 10 minutes at the same temperature. Remove from the oven, scatter over the walnuts and serve with a mixed salad.

cheese & vegetable pasties

easy

serves 4

20 minutes + 40 minutes to chill

50 minutes

ingredients

PASTRY
225 g/8 oz plain wholemeal flour, plus extra for dusting
pinch of salt
100 g/3½ oz butter, diced, plus extra for greasing
4 tbsp cold water
2 tbsp milk, for glazing

FILLING
25 g/1 oz butter
1 onion, chopped
125 g/4½ oz potatoes, chopped
100 g/3½ oz carrots, chopped
25 g/1 oz French beans, chopped
100 ml/3½ fl oz water
2 tbsp canned and drained sweetcorn kernels
1 tbsp chopped fresh parsley
60 g/2¼ oz Cheddar cheese, grated
salt and pepper

To make the pastry, sift the flour and salt into a large bowl. Rub in the butter until the mixture resembles breadcrumbs. Add the water and mix to a dough. Cover with clingfilm. Refrigerate for 40 minutes.

To make the filling, melt the butter in a large saucepan over a low heat. Add the onion, potatoes and carrots and cook, stirring, for 5 minutes. Add the French beans and water. Bring to the boil, reduce the heat and simmer for 15 minutes. Remove from the heat, drain, rinse under cold running water, then drain again. Leave to cool.

Preheat the oven to 200°C/400°F/Gas Mark 6. Cut the pastry into quarters and roll out on a floured work surface into 4 circles about 15 cm/6 inches in diameter. Mix the vegetables with the sweetcorn, parsley, cheese, and salt and pepper to taste. Spoon on to one half of each pastry circle. Brush the edges with water, then fold over and press together. Transfer to a greased baking tray. Brush all over with milk. Bake in the preheated oven for 30 minutes until golden.

country cheese pies

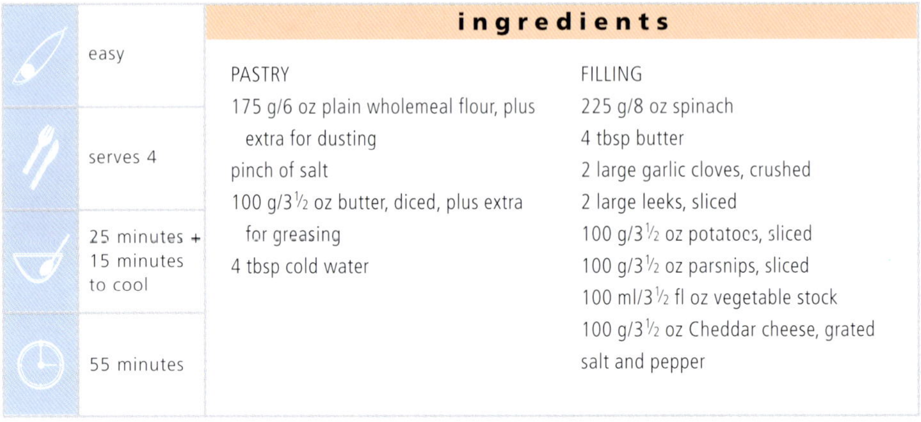

easy

serves 4

25 minutes + 15 minutes to cool

55 minutes

ingredients

PASTRY

175 g/6 oz plain wholemeal flour, plus extra for dusting
pinch of salt
100 g/3½ oz butter, diced, plus extra for greasing
4 tbsp cold water

FILLING

225 g/8 oz spinach
4 tbsp butter
2 large garlic cloves, crushed
2 large leeks, sliced
100 g/3½ oz potatoes, sliced
100 g/3½ oz parsnips, sliced
100 ml/3½ fl oz vegetable stock
100 g/3½ oz Cheddar cheese, grated
salt and pepper

To make the filling, rinse the spinach, put into a saucepan and cook with just the water clinging to the leaves for 5 minutes until wilted. Drain and leave until cool enough to handle. Squeeze out the excess liquid. Melt the butter in a large saucepan over a medium heat, add the garlic and leeks and cook, stirring, for 3 minutes. Add the potatoes and parsnips and cook for 7 minutes. Add the stock, bring to the boil, then simmer for 15 minutes. Drain and leave to cool.

Preheat the oven to 200°C/400°F/Gas Mark 6. Sift the flour and salt into a bowl. Rub in the butter until the mixture resembles breadcrumbs. Stir in the water, mix to a dough, then cut in half. On a floured work surface, roll out one half into 4 circles 13 cm/5 inches in diameter. Use to line 4 greased tartlet tins. Roll out the other half into 4 slightly larger circles. Mix the vegetables with the spinach, cheese and seasoning and divide among the pastry cases. Brush the edges with water. Cover with the pastry circles, seal and crimp the edges. Pierce the tops with a fork. Bake for 25 minutes until golden.

red onion tartlets

easy	
serves 4	
35 minutes + 40 minutes to chill	
40 minutes	

ingredients

PASTRY

100 g/3½ oz plain white or wholemeal flour, plus extra for dusting
pinch of salt
85 g/3 oz butter, diced, plus extra for greasing
2 tbsp cold water

FILLING

15 g/½ oz butter
1 garlic clove, crushed
2 red onions, finely sliced
1 egg, beaten
125 ml/4 fl oz double cream
60 g/2¼ oz Parmesan cheese, grated
salt and pepper

To make the pastry, sift the flour and salt into a bowl. Rub in the butter until the mixture resembles breadcrumbs. Stir in the water, mix to a dough, then use your hands to shape the dough into a ball. Cover with clingfilm and refrigerate for 40 minutes. Meanwhile, melt the butter in a small frying pan over a low heat. Add the garlic and onions and cook, stirring, for 4–5 minutes until softened. Remove from the heat and leave to cool.

Preheat the oven to 180°C/350°F/Gas Mark 4. Remove the dough from the refrigerator and roll out on a floured work surface. Using a 10-cm/4-inch round biscuit cutter, cut out 12 circles and use them to line 12 greased, deep fluted patty tins. Trim the pastry.

Put the egg, cream and cheese into a bowl and whisk together. Add the onions and season with salt and pepper to taste. Divide the filling between the pastry cases, then bake in the preheated oven for 35 minutes until golden. Remove from the oven and serve hot or cold.

salmon morsels

extremely easy	
serves 4	
15 minutes	
15 minutes	

ingredients

2 crusty baguettes or 1 French stick
3 tbsp olive oil
200 g/7 oz cream cheese
1 tbsp snipped fresh chives
1 tbsp finely grated lemon rind
100 g/3½ oz smoked salmon slices, cut into strips

lemon wedges, to serve

Preheat the oven to 180°C/350°F/Gas Mark 4. Using a sharp knife, cut the bread into thick slices. Drizzle with oil, transfer to an ovenproof dish and bake in the preheated oven for 15 minutes.

Meanwhile, to make the topping, put the cream cheese into a bowl and add the chives and grated lemon rind. Mix together well.

Remove the bread slices from the oven and leave to cool. Spread a thick layer of the cream cheese mixture on one side of each bread slice, arrange strips of smoked salmon on the top and serve with lemon wedges.

fragrant chicken parcels

very easy	
serves 4	
20 minutes	
35 minutes	

ingredients

- 1 tbsp olive oil
- 150 g/5½ oz Cheddar cheese, grated
- 1 garlic clove, crushed
- 1 tbsp chopped fresh flat-leaved parsley
- 4 skinless, boneless chicken breasts
- 150 g/5½ oz button mushrooms, sliced
- 4 tomatoes, halved and sliced
- 1 leek, sliced
- salt and pepper
- 2 tbsp white wine

sprigs of fresh flat-leaved parsley, to garnish

freshly cooked rice, to serve

Preheat the oven to 200°C/400°F/Gas Mark 6. Cut 4 squares of foil, each measuring about 25 cm/10 inches across. Brush each foil square with oil and arrange in a roasting dish. Pull up the edges of each square a little to make them into shallow 'bowls'.

Put the cheese, garlic and parsley into a bowl and mix together well. Using a sharp knife, make a long slit in each chicken breast, then fill each cut with the cheese mixture. Close the edges.

Divide the mushrooms, tomatoes and leek between the foil pieces, then place a chicken breast on top of each pile of vegetables. Season to taste with salt and pepper, then sprinkle over the wine. Bring the edges of the foil over the chicken and vegetables and close tightly to enclose the contents within the parcels. Transfer to the preheated oven and bake for 35 minutes, or until the chicken is cooked through and the vegetables are tender. Remove from the oven. Serve in the foil, garnished with parsley sprigs, with rice.

cheese & ham pizzas

easy	
serves 4	
20 minutes + 40 minutes to rise/cool	
50–55 minutes	

ingredients

PIZZA BASES
350 g/12 oz plain flour, plus extra for dusting
7 g/¼ oz easy-blend dried yeast
1 tsp salt
1 tbsp extra-virgin olive oil, plus extra for brushing
250 ml/9 fl oz lukewarm water

TOPPING
1 tbsp olive oil, plus extra for drizzling
2 garlic cloves, crushed
800 g/1 lb 12 oz canned chopped plum tomatoes
1 tbsp tomato purée
275 g/9½ oz mozzarella cheese, diced
225 g/8 oz lean ham, cut into small pieces
125 g/4½ oz mushrooms, sliced
salt and pepper
fresh basil leaves, to garnish

To make the bases, mix together the flour, yeast and salt in a bowl. Make a well in the centre and stir in the oil and enough of the water to make a smooth dough. Knead on a lightly floured work surface for 5 minutes. Wash the bowl and brush with oil. Shape the dough into a ball and return to the bowl. Cover with clingfilm. Leave to rise for 30 minutes or until doubled in size. Knead the dough for another 2–3 minutes, return to the bowl and cover again.

Meanwhile, heat the oil in a large frying pan over a medium heat and cook the garlic, stirring, for 3 minutes. Add the tomatoes and tomato purée and cook for 20–25 minutes, or until thickened. Leave to cool.

Preheat the oven to 200°C/400°F/Gas Mark 6. Divide the dough into 4 pieces, shape into balls, then roll out into flat circles 5 mm/¼ inch thick. Spread over the tomato sauce. Top with mozzarella, ham and mushrooms. Add salt and pepper to taste, then drizzle with oil. Bake for 25 minutes and serve garnished with basil leaves.

steamed vegetables en papillotes

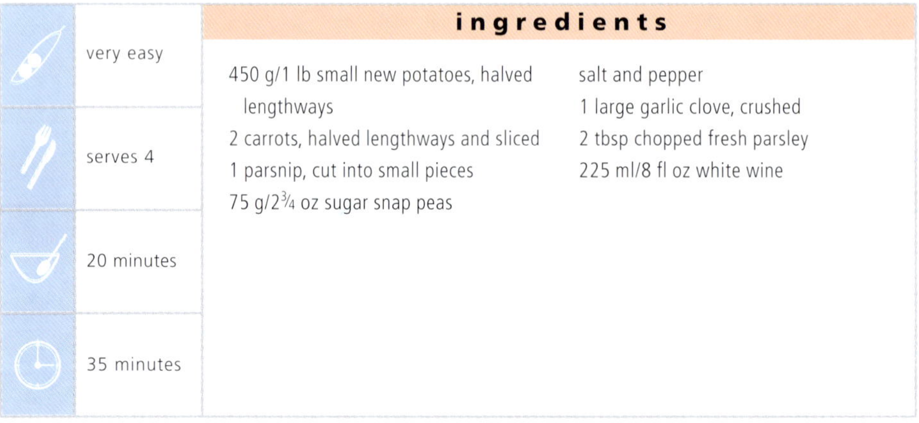

very easy	
serves 4	
20 minutes	
35 minutes	

ingredients

450 g/1 lb small new potatoes, halved lengthways
2 carrots, halved lengthways and sliced
1 parsnip, cut into small pieces
75 g/2¾ oz sugar snap peas
salt and pepper
1 large garlic clove, crushed
2 tbsp chopped fresh parsley
225 ml/8 fl oz white wine

Preheat the oven to 200°C/400°F/Gas Mark 6. Fill a large saucepan with water and bring to the boil. Blanch the potatoes, carrots and parsnip in the boiling water for 2 minutes. Drain, rinse under cold running water, then drain again. Set aside.

Cut 4 squares of greaseproof paper, each measuring about 25 cm/ 10 inches across, and arrange in a roasting dish. Scrunch up the edges of each square a little to make them into shallow 'bowls', then divide the blanched vegetables between them. Top with the sugar snap peas and season to taste with salt and pepper.

In a bowl, mix the garlic with the parsley, then stir in the wine. Pour the mixture over the vegetables. Bring the edges of the paper over the vegetables and close tightly to enclose the contents within the parcels. Transfer to the preheated oven and bake for 30 minutes, or until the vegetables are tender. Remove from the oven and serve in the parcels.

stuffed tomatoes

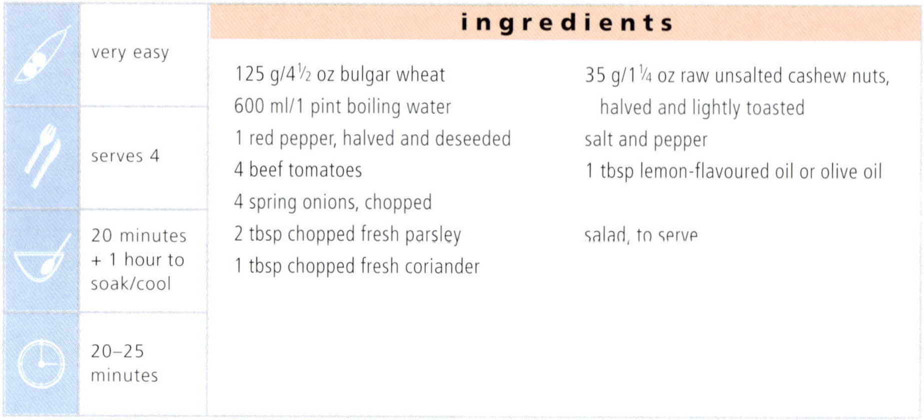

very easy

serves 4

20 minutes + 1 hour to soak/cool

20–25 minutes

ingredients

125 g/4½ oz bulgar wheat
600 ml/1 pint boiling water
1 red pepper, halved and deseeded
4 beef tomatoes
4 spring onions, chopped
2 tbsp chopped fresh parsley
1 tbsp chopped fresh coriander
35 g/1¼ oz raw unsalted cashew nuts, halved and lightly toasted
salt and pepper
1 tbsp lemon-flavoured oil or olive oil

salad, to serve

Put the bulgar wheat into a heatproof bowl and cover with the boiling water. Leave to soak for 1 hour, or until most of the water has been absorbed. Meanwhile, cut the red pepper pieces in half to give 4 quarters. Arrange them, skin side up, on a grill rack and cook under a preheated medium–hot grill for 10 minutes, or until the skins are evenly blackened. Remove from the grill, place in a polythene bag and set aside for 15 minutes. When cool enough to handle, remove and discard the skins. Chop the flesh.

Cut the tomatoes in half, scoop out the seeds and discard. Drain the wheat thoroughly and place in a large bowl. Add the spring onions, parsley, coriander, nuts and red pepper. Season to taste with salt and pepper and mix together well. Spoon the mixture into the tomato shells and transfer them to a grill rack covered with foil. Drizzle over the oil and cook under a preheated medium–hot grill for 10–15 minutes, or until the tomatoes are tender. Serve hot with a salad.

classic roast potatoes

very easy	**ingredients**
serves 4	900 g/2 lb medium-large floury potatoes, peeled ½ tsp salt pepper paprika 100 ml/3½ fl oz vegetable oil
10 minutes	
1½ hours	

Preheat the oven to 200°C/400°F/Gas Mark 6. Using a sharp knife, cut the potatoes in half, or into quarters if very large, then arrange in a roasting tin. Sprinkle over the salt, then season to taste with pepper and paprika.

Pour the oil over the potatoes, then turn them in the oil until thoroughly coated. Transfer to the preheated oven and roast, basting occasionally, for 1½ hours, or until golden brown and tender. Remove from the oven and serve at once.

To ring the changes, try adding 1 crushed garlic clove and 1 tablespoon of lemon juice to the oil before pouring over the potatoes. They will add a deliciously different flavour and the aroma will be irresistible.

main dishes

The recipes in this chapter are truly inspirational and mouthwatering. The Grilled Trout Fillets, and the Salmon Steaks with Lime Salsa will delight fish lovers everywhere, and the meat and poultry dishes will satisfy every taste. From Traditional Roast Chicken, or Maple Roast Lamb with Cider, to Stuffed Roast Pork with Garlic, each dish uses deliciously fresh and succulent ingredients. And the vegetarian dishes are hard to beat. You will find the Baked Vegetable Crumble and Mushroom Risotto every bit as exciting and satisfying as the meat dishes.

baked vegetable crumble

easy	
serves 4	
25 minutes	
1 hour	

ingredients

VEGETABLE FILLING
40 g/1½ oz butter
1 garlic clove, crushed
1 large leek, sliced
100 g/3½ oz potatoes, chopped
100 g/3½ oz carrots, chopped
85 g/3 oz parsnips, chopped
85 g/3 oz small broccoli florets
225 g/8 oz tomatoes, cut into eighths
25 g/1 oz wholemeal flour
100 ml/3½ fl oz milk
200 ml/7 fl oz vegetable stock
1 tbsp chopped fresh parsley
1 tbsp chopped fresh thyme
salt and pepper

CRUMBLE TOPPING
115 g/4 oz wholemeal flour
75 g/2¾ oz butter
75 g/2¾ oz Cheddar cheese, grated
25 g/1 oz walnuts, finely chopped
25 g/1 oz ground almonds
1 tbsp chopped fresh thyme

To make the filling, melt the butter in a large saucepan over a low heat, add the garlic and leek and cook, stirring, for 4 minutes until softened. Add the potatoes, carrots, parsnips, broccoli and tomatoes and cook, stirring occasionally, for 12–15 minutes. Stir in the flour and cook for 1 minute. Remove from the heat and gradually stir in the milk and stock. Return to the heat and cook, stirring, until thickened. Add the herbs and seasoning. Simmer for 20 minutes.

Meanwhile, to make the crumble, put the flour into a large bowl, then rub in the butter until the mixture resembles breadcrumbs. Add the cheese, walnuts, almonds and thyme and mix well. Preheat the oven to 200°C/400°F/Gas Mark 6.

Remove the vegetable mixture from the heat and transfer to an ovenproof dish. Spoon the crumble over the top and press down gently. Bake in the preheated oven for 25 minutes, or until golden and the vegetables are cooked through. Serve hot.

vegetable pasta with tofu

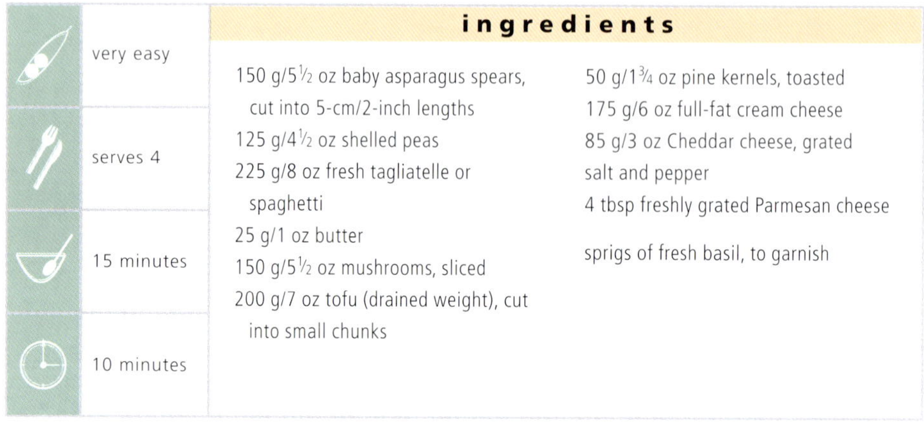

very easy

serves 4

15 minutes

10 minutes

ingredients

150 g/5½ oz baby asparagus spears, cut into 5-cm/2-inch lengths
125 g/4½ oz shelled peas
225 g/8 oz fresh tagliatelle or spaghetti
25 g/1 oz butter
150 g/5½ oz mushrooms, sliced
200 g/7 oz tofu (drained weight), cut into small chunks
50 g/1¾ oz pine kernels, toasted
175 g/6 oz full-fat cream cheese
85 g/3 oz Cheddar cheese, grated
salt and pepper
4 tbsp freshly grated Parmesan cheese

sprigs of fresh basil, to garnish

Bring two large saucepans of lightly salted water to the boil. Add the asparagus and peas to one saucepan and cook for 3 minutes. Drain, rinse under cold running water, then drain again. Put the pasta into the other saucepan and cook for 3–4 minutes, or until tender but still firm to the bite.

While the pasta is cooking, melt the butter in a large frying pan over a medium heat. Add the mushrooms and tofu and cook, stirring, for 2 minutes. Add the pine kernels, asparagus and peas, then stir in the cream cheese and Cheddar cheese and season to taste with salt and pepper. Cook for another 2 minutes.

Drain the pasta and divide among serving plates. Remove the vegetable and tofu sauce from the heat and spoon it over the pasta. Scatter over the freshly grated Parmesan cheese. Garnish with basil sprigs and serve immediately.

mushroom risotto

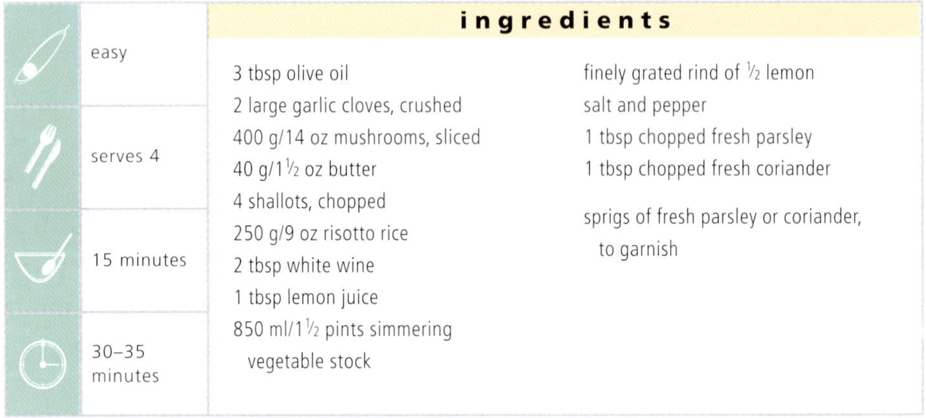

easy	
serves 4	
15 minutes	
30–35 minutes	

ingredients

3 tbsp olive oil
2 large garlic cloves, crushed
400 g/14 oz mushrooms, sliced
40 g/1 ½ oz butter
4 shallots, chopped
250 g/9 oz risotto rice
2 tbsp white wine
1 tbsp lemon juice
850 ml/1 ½ pints simmering vegetable stock
finely grated rind of ½ lemon
salt and pepper
1 tbsp chopped fresh parsley
1 tbsp chopped fresh coriander

sprigs of fresh parsley or coriander, to garnish

Heat the oil in a large frying pan over a low heat, add the garlic and mushrooms and cook, stirring, for 3 minutes. Remove from the heat and set aside.

Heat the butter in a large saucepan over a medium heat, add the shallots and cook, stirring, for 3 minutes. Add the rice and cook, stirring constantly, for 2 minutes, then pour in the wine and lemon juice and stir until the liquid is almost absorbed. Add a ladleful of the simmering stock, and cook, stirring, until it is absorbed. Keep adding the stock, a ladleful at a time, waiting for each ladleful to be absorbed before adding the next. When all the liquid has almost been absorbed, stir in the mushrooms, lemon rind, and salt and pepper to taste. Continue to cook, stirring, until the liquid has been completely absorbed, then remove from the heat and stir in the parsley and coriander. Serve immediately, garnished with parsley or coriander sprigs.

grilled trout fillets

very easy	
serves 4	
20 minutes	
5 minutes	

ingredients

2 tbsp chopped toasted hazelnuts
2 tbsp ground almonds
115 g/4 oz Cheddar cheese, grated
4 tbsp fresh breadcrumbs, white or wholemeal
1 egg
1 tbsp milk
salt and pepper

4 organic brown trout fillets, about 175 g/6 oz each
2 tbsp plain flour

sprigs of fresh flat-leaved parsley, to garnish

freshly cooked rice, to serve

Preheat the grill to medium. Put the hazelnuts and almonds into a bowl, add the cheese and breadcrumbs and mix together. In a separate bowl, beat together the egg and milk. Season to taste with salt and pepper.

Rinse the fish fillets and pat dry with kitchen paper. Coat the fillets in the flour, then dip them into the egg mixture. Transfer them to the bowl containing the nuts and cheese, and turn the fillets in the mixture until thoroughly coated.

Cook the fish under the preheated grill for 5 minutes, turning once during the cooking time, or until golden and cooked through. Remove from the grill and transfer to serving plates. Garnish with parsley sprigs and serve with freshly cooked rice.

salmon steaks with lime salsa

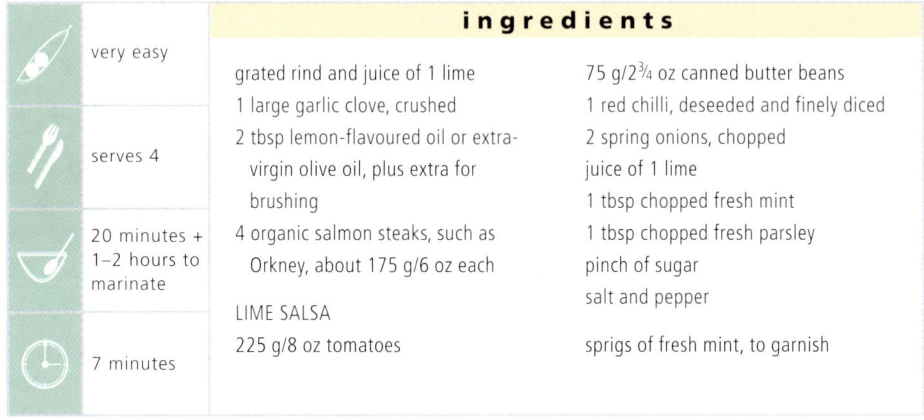

very easy

serves 4

20 minutes + 1–2 hours to marinate

7 minutes

ingredients

grated rind and juice of 1 lime
1 large garlic clove, crushed
2 tbsp lemon-flavoured oil or extra-virgin olive oil, plus extra for brushing
4 organic salmon steaks, such as Orkney, about 175 g/6 oz each

LIME SALSA
225 g/8 oz tomatoes
75 g/2¾ oz canned butter beans
1 red chilli, deseeded and finely diced
2 spring onions, chopped
juice of 1 lime
1 tbsp chopped fresh mint
1 tbsp chopped fresh parsley
pinch of sugar
salt and pepper

sprigs of fresh mint, to garnish

Put the lime rind and juice into a large, shallow, non-metallic dish that will not react with acid, such as ceramic or glass. Add the garlic and the oil and stir together well. Remove any bones from the fish, rinse the steaks under cold running water and pat dry with kitchen paper. Transfer to the dish and coat in the mixture. Cover with clingfilm and refrigerate for 1–2 hours.

Meanwhile, to make the salsa, put the tomatoes in a heatproof bowl and cover with boiling water. Soak for 3–4 minutes, remove from the water and cool slightly. When cool enough to handle, pierce the skins with the point of a knife. Remove the skins, halve the tomatoes and remove the seeds. Chop the flesh and transfer to a bowl. Mix in the remaining ingredients, cover with clingfilm and refrigerate for 1 hour.

Preheat the grill to high, cover the grill rack with foil and brush with oil. Grill the fish for 7 minutes, turning once. Do not overcook. Garnish with mint sprigs and serve with the salsa.

traditional roast chicken

easy	
serves 4	
20 minutes + 10 minutes to rest	
1 hour 50 minutes	

ingredients

25 g/1 oz butter, softened
1 garlic clove, finely chopped
3 tbsp finely chopped toasted walnuts
1 tbsp chopped fresh parsley
salt and pepper
1 medium oven-ready chicken, weighing 1.8 kg/4 lb
1 lime, cut into quarters
2 tbsp vegetable oil
1 tbsp cornflour
2 tbsp water

TO GARNISH
lime wedges
sprigs of fresh rosemary

TO SERVE
Classic Roast Potatoes (see page 52)
selection of freshly cooked vegetables

Preheat the oven to 190°C/375°F/Gas Mark 5. In a small bowl, mix 1 tablespoon of the butter with the garlic, walnuts and parsley. Season well. Loosen the skin from the breast of the chicken without breaking it. Spread the butter mixture evenly between the skin and breast meat. Put the lime quarters inside the body cavity.

Pour the oil into a roasting tin. Transfer the chicken to the tin and dot the skin with the remaining butter. Roast for 1¾ hours, basting occasionally, until the chicken is tender and the juices run clear when a skewer is inserted into the thickest part of the meat. Lift out and place on a serving platter to rest for 10 minutes.

Blend the cornflour with the water, then stir into the juices in the tin. Transfer to the stove. Stir over a low heat until thickened. Add more water if necessary. Garnish the chicken with lime wedges and rosemary sprigs. Serve with Classic Roast Potatoes, a selection of cooked vegetables and the thickened juices.

chicken & potato pie

very easy	
serves 4	
25 minutes + 1 hour to chill	
1 1/4 hours	

ingredients

PASTRY
350 g/12 oz plain flour
pinch of salt
175 g/6 oz butter, diced
about 6 tbsp cold water
milk, for brushing

FILLING
250 ml/9 fl oz chicken stock
700 g/1 lb 9 oz boneless, skinless chicken, cut into bite-sized chunks
100 g/3 1/2 oz potatoes, roughly chopped
1 egg, beaten
75 g/2 3/4 oz hazelnuts, toasted and ground
75 g/2 3/4 oz Cheddar cheese, grated
2 spring onions, chopped
1 tbsp chopped fresh sage
salt and pepper

selection of freshly cooked vegetables, to serve

To make the pastry, sift the flour and salt into a bowl. Rub in the butter until the mixture resembles breadcrumbs. Gradually stir in enough of the cold water to make a pliable dough. Knead lightly. Cover with clingfilm and refrigerate for 1 hour. Meanwhile, bring the stock to the boil in a saucepan. Reduce the heat, add the chicken and potatoes and simmer for 30 minutes. Remove from the heat, cool for 25 minutes, then drain off the liquid and transfer the chicken and potatoes to a bowl. Stir in the remaining ingredients.

Preheat the oven to 190°C/375°F/Gas Mark 5. Grease a 23-cm/9-inch pie tin with butter. Remove the dough from the refrigerator. On a floured work surface, shape into a ball, roll out half of the dough to a thickness of 5 mm/1/4 inch and use to line the tin. Spoon in the filling. Roll out the remaining pastry to make the lid. Brush the pie rim with water, cover with the lid and trim the edges. Cut 2 slits in the top. Add decorative shapes made from dough trimmings. Brush with milk. Bake for 45 minutes, then serve with vegetables.

maple roast lamb with cider

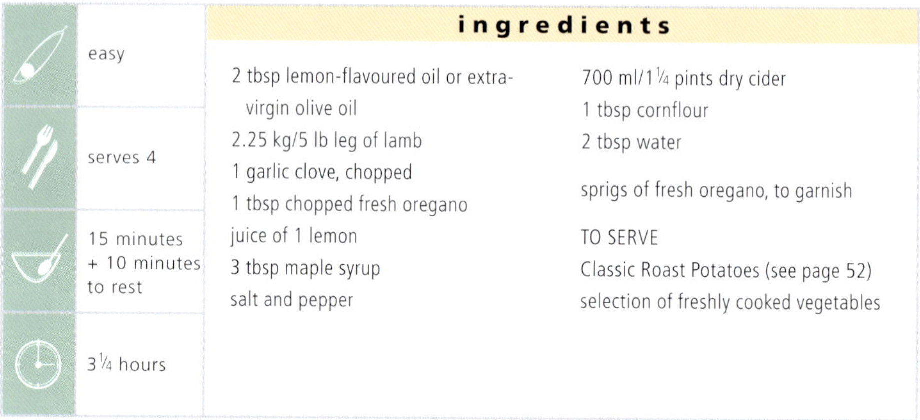

easy

serves 4

15 minutes + 10 minutes to rest

3¼ hours

ingredients

2 tbsp lemon-flavoured oil or extra-virgin olive oil
2.25 kg/5 lb leg of lamb
1 garlic clove, chopped
1 tbsp chopped fresh oregano
juice of 1 lemon
3 tbsp maple syrup
salt and pepper

700 ml/1¼ pints dry cider
1 tbsp cornflour
2 tbsp water

sprigs of fresh oregano, to garnish

TO SERVE
Classic Roast Potatoes (see page 52)
selection of freshly cooked vegetables

Preheat the oven to 200°C/400°F/Gas Mark 6. Pour the oil into a roasting tin. Using a sharp knife, trim off and discard any excess fat from the lamb, then make small incisions all over. Transfer the joint to the roasting tin. Put the garlic into a bowl and add the chopped oregano, lemon juice, maple syrup, and salt and pepper to taste. Mix together well. Pour the mixture evenly over the lamb, pushing it into the incisions, then pour over the cider.

Transfer the tin to the preheated oven and roast for 30 minutes, turning once and basting occasionally. Reduce the oven temperature to 150°C/300°F/Gas Mark 2 and cook for a further 2¾ hours, or until tender and cooked through. Lift out and place on a serving platter to rest for 10 minutes. Blend the cornflour with the water, then stir into the juices in the tin. Transfer to the stove. Stir over a low heat until thickened. Garnish the lamb with oregano sprigs. Serve with Classic Roast Potatoes, vegetables and the thickened juices.

stuffed roast pork with garlic

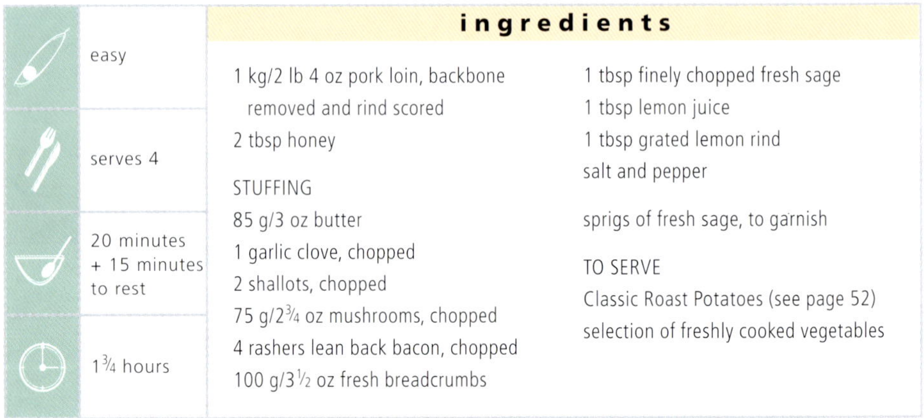

easy

serves 4

20 minutes + 15 minutes to rest

1¾ hours

ingredients

1 kg/2 lb 4 oz pork loin, backbone removed and rind scored
2 tbsp honey

STUFFING
85 g/3 oz butter
1 garlic clove, chopped
2 shallots, chopped
75 g/2¾ oz mushrooms, chopped
4 rashers lean back bacon, chopped
100 g/3½ oz fresh breadcrumbs
1 tbsp finely chopped fresh sage
1 tbsp lemon juice
1 tbsp grated lemon rind
salt and pepper

sprigs of fresh sage, to garnish

TO SERVE
Classic Roast Potatoes (see page 52)
selection of freshly cooked vegetables

Preheat the oven to 230°C/450°F/Gas Mark 8. To make the stuffing, melt the butter in a saucepan over a medium heat. Add the garlic and shallots and cook, stirring, for 3 minutes, or until softened. Add the mushrooms and bacon, and cook for another 2 minutes. Remove from the heat and stir in the breadcrumbs, sage, lemon juice and rind, and salt and pepper to taste.

Put the stuffing in the middle of the pork loin, then roll up and secure the loin with several lengths of tied string. Place the joint in a roasting tin, then rub the skin with plenty of salt and season with pepper. Brush the honey over the pork.

Cook in the preheated oven for 25 minutes, then reduce the heat to 180°C/350°F/Gas Mark 4. Cook, basting occasionally, for about 1¼ hours, or until cooked through. Remove from the oven and leave to rest for 15 minutes. Garnish with sage sprigs and serve with Classic Roast Potatoes and vegetables.

beef & vegetable stir-fry

very easy	
serves 4	
15 minutes	
5 minutes	

ingredients

500 g/1 lb 2 oz beef fillet
2 tbsp vegetable oil
1 garlic clove, chopped
2 spring onions, sliced
1 red pepper, deseeded and sliced
1 green pepper, deseeded and sliced
3 tbsp unsalted cashew nuts
1 tbsp lime juice
1 tbsp red wine
salt and pepper
1 tbsp chopped fresh coriander

freshly cooked noodles or rice, to serve

Cut the beef across the grain into long, thin strips. Heat the oil in a wok or large frying pan over a high heat. Add the garlic and spring onions and stir-fry for 1 minute. Add the beef and stir-fry for 1 minute.

Add the red and green peppers and the cashew nuts, then stir in the lime juice and wine. Season to taste with salt and pepper and stir-fry for another 3 minutes. Scatter over the coriander. Remove from the heat. Serve with freshly cooked noodles or rice.

desserts

What organic cookbook would be complete without a selection of sumptuous desserts? Within the following pages you will find recipes for every occasion, from juicy Baked Apples in Red Wine, and Fruit Kebabs with Chocolate Sauce, to a satisfying Apple Lattice Tart and a tantalising Peach & Strawberry Meringue. Chocolate lovers will adore the Chocolate Cups, and what better way to round off a meal than a fragrant Tropical Fruit Salad served with double cream? The cakes in this section also make irresistible desserts, or are wonderful served with coffee at any time of day.

baked apples in red wine

very easy

serves 4

15 minutes

40–45 minutes

ingredients

4 medium cooking apples
1 tbsp lemon juice
50 g/1¾ oz blueberries
50 g/1¾ oz raisins
25 g/1 oz chopped toasted mixed nuts
½ tsp ground cinnamon
2 tbsp soft brown sugar
275 ml/9½ fl oz red wine
2 tsp cornflour
4 tsp water

double cream, to serve

Preheat the oven to 200°C/400°F/Gas Mark 6. Using a sharp knife, score a line around the centre of each apple. Core the apples, then brush the centres with lemon juice to prevent discolouration. Transfer them to a small roasting tin.

Put the blueberries and raisins into a bowl, then add the nuts, cinnamon and sugar. Mix together well. Spoon the mixture into the centre of each apple, then pour over the wine.

Transfer the stuffed apples to the preheated oven and bake for 40–45 minutes, or until tender. Remove from the oven, then lift out the apples and keep them warm.

Blend the cornflour with the water, then add the mixture to the cooking juices in the roasting tin. Transfer to the stove and cook over a medium heat, stirring, until thickened. Remove from the heat and pour over the apples. Serve with double cream.

apple lattice tart

easy	
serves 4	
20 minutes + 1 hour to chill	
50 minutes	

ingredients

PASTRY
300 g/10½ oz plain flour, plus extra for dusting
pinch of salt
50 g/1¾ oz caster sugar
250 g/9 oz butter, diced
1 whole egg plus 1 egg yolk
about 1 tbsp water

FILLING
3 tbsp blackcurrant or plum jam
60 g/2¼ oz chopped toasted mixed nuts
950 g/2 lb 2 oz cooking apples
1 tbsp lemon juice
1 tsp ground mixed spice
60 g/2¼ oz sultanas
50 g/1¾ oz grapes, halved and deseeded
70 g/2½ oz soft brown sugar
icing sugar, for dusting

custard, to serve

To make the pastry, sift the flour and salt into a bowl. Make a well in the centre and add the sugar, butter, egg, egg yolk and water. Mix together to form a smooth dough, adding more water if necessary. Cover with clingfilm and refrigerate for 1 hour. Preheat the oven to 200°C/400°F/Gas Mark 6. Shape three-quarters of the dough into a ball and roll out on a floured work surface into a circle large enough to line a shallow 25-cm/10-inch flan tin. Trim the edges. Roll out the remaining pastry and cut into long strips about 1-cm/½-inch wide.

To make the filling, spread the jam over the base of the pastry case, then sprinkle over the nuts. Peel and core the apples, then cut into thin slices. Put them into a bowl with the lemon juice, mixed spice, sultanas, grapes and brown sugar. Mix together gently. Spoon the mixture into the pastry case, then arrange the pastry strips in a lattice over the top. Moisten with water, seal and trim the edges. Bake for 50 minutes until golden. Dust with icing sugar. Serve with custard.

fruit kebabs with chocolate sauce

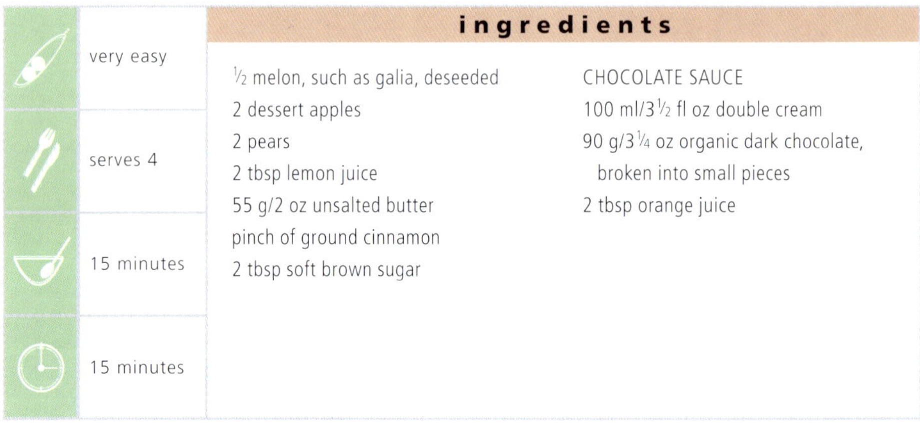

very easy

serves 4

15 minutes

15 minutes

ingredients

- ½ melon, such as galia, deseeded
- 2 dessert apples
- 2 pears
- 2 tbsp lemon juice
- 55 g/2 oz unsalted butter
- pinch of ground cinnamon
- 2 tbsp soft brown sugar

CHOCOLATE SAUCE

- 100 ml/3½ fl oz double cream
- 90 g/3¼ oz organic dark chocolate, broken into small pieces
- 2 tbsp orange juice

Cut the melon flesh into small chunks and put into a bowl. Core the apples and pears, cut into small chunks and add to the bowl with the lemon juice. Stir together gently. Put the butter into a saucepan and melt gently over a low heat. Stir in the cinnamon and sugar, then remove from the heat and pour into a large, shallow dish. Thread the melon on to skewers, alternating with pieces of apple and pear. When the skewers are full (leave a small space at either end), turn them in the spiced butter mixture until thoroughly coated.

To make the sauce, pour the cream into a small saucepan and bring gently to the boil over a low heat. Remove from the heat, add the chocolate and stir until melted. Stir in the orange juice and keep warm until required.

Cook the kebabs under a preheated medium grill, turning frequently, for 10 minutes, or until tender. Remove from the grill and serve immediately with the warm chocolate sauce.

summer fruit pudding

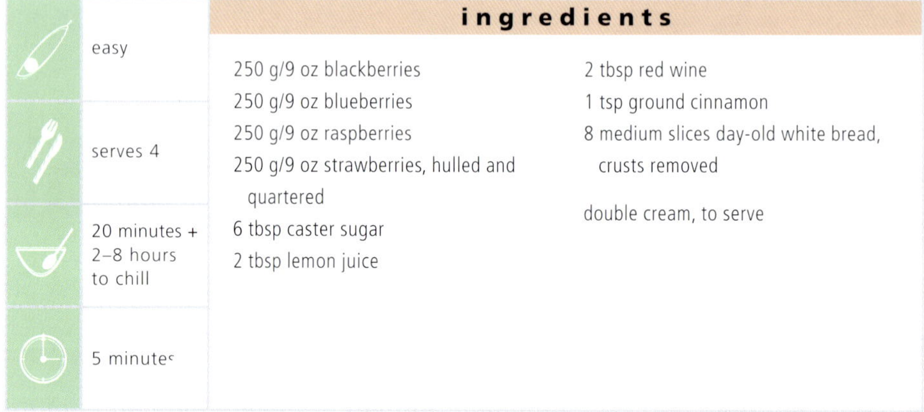

easy

serves 4

20 minutes + 2–8 hours to chill

5 minutes

ingredients

250 g/9 oz blackberries
250 g/9 oz blueberries
250 g/9 oz raspberries
250 g/9 oz strawberries, hulled and quartered
6 tbsp caster sugar
2 tbsp lemon juice
2 tbsp red wine
1 tsp ground cinnamon
8 medium slices day-old white bread, crusts removed

double cream, to serve

Put the blackberries, blueberries, raspberries and strawberries into a large saucepan over a medium heat. Add the sugar, lemon juice, wine and cinnamon. Heat for 5 minutes, stirring gently, until the sugar has dissolved. Remove from the heat and leave to cool.

Cut the bread slices diagonally into quarters, then use them to line the bottom and sides of an 850-ml/1½-pint pudding basin, reserving a few pieces to cover. Spoon the berry mixture into the pudding basin and cover with the remaining bread. Put the basin inside a shallow bowl to catch any juices and top with a small plate that fits snugly inside the basin's rim. Put a heavy can of food on top to weigh down the plate, then refrigerate for at least 2 hours, or overnight if possible.

Remove the can and the plate, and use a knife to loosen the sides of the pudding. Turn out on to a serving plate and serve with double cream.

carrot cake

very easy

makes 6

20 minutes + 40 minutes to cool

55 minutes

ingredients

butter, for greasing
100 g/3½ oz self-raising flour
pinch of salt
1 tsp ground mixed spice
½ tsp ground nutmeg
125 g/4½ oz soft brown sugar
2 eggs, beaten
5 tbsp sunflower oil
125 g/4½ oz carrots, peeled and grated
1 banana, chopped
25 g/1 oz chopped toasted mixed nuts

ICING
40 g/1½ oz butter, softened
3 tbsp cream cheese
175 g/6 oz icing sugar, sifted
1 tsp orange juice
grated rind of ½ orange

walnut halves or pieces, to decorate

Preheat the oven to 190°C/375°F/Gas Mark 5. Grease an 18-cm/7-inch square cake tin with butter and line with baking paper. Sift the flour, salt, mixed spice and nutmeg into a bowl. Stir in the brown sugar, then stir in the eggs and oil. Add the carrots, banana and chopped mixed nuts and mix together well.

Spoon the mixture into the prepared cake tin and level the surface. Transfer to the preheated oven and bake for 55 minutes, or until golden and just firm to the touch. Remove from the oven and leave to cool. When cool enough to handle, turn out on to a wire rack and leave to cool completely.

To make the icing, put the butter, cream cheese, icing sugar, and orange juice and rind into a bowl and beat together until creamy. Spread the icing over the top of the cold cake, then use a fork to make shallow wavy lines in the icing. Scatter over the walnuts, cut the cake into bars and serve.

coffee & walnut cake

easy	
serves 4	
20 minutes + 2½ hours to cool/chill	
1 hour	

ingredients

ICING
6 tbsp organic cocoa powder
2 tbsp cornflour
6 tbsp caster sugar
125 ml/4 fl oz strong black coffee, cooled
250 ml/9 fl oz milk

SPONGE
275 g/9½ oz plain flour
1 tbsp baking powder
85 g/3 oz caster sugar
85 g/3 oz butter, softened, plus extra for greasing
2 eggs
150 ml/5 fl oz milk
3 tbsp hot strong black coffee
60 g/2¼ oz shelled walnuts, chopped
50 g/1¾ oz sultanas

walnut halves, to decorate

To make the icing, put all the ingredients into a food processor and process until creamy. Transfer to a saucepan and heat, stirring, over a medium heat until bubbling. Cook for 1 minute, then pour into a heatproof bowl. Leave to cool, then cover with clingfilm and refrigerate for at least 2 hours.

Preheat the oven to 190°C/375°F/Gas Mark 5. Grease a 23-cm/ 9-inch loose-bottomed cake tin with butter and line with baking paper. To make the sponge, sift the flour and baking powder into a bowl, then stir in the sugar. In a separate bowl, beat together the butter, eggs, milk and coffee, then mix into the flour mixture. Stir in the chopped walnuts and the sultanas. Spoon the mixture into the prepared cake tin and level the surface. Transfer to the preheated oven and bake for 1 hour. Remove from the oven and leave to cool. When cool enough to handle, turn out on to a wire rack and leave to cool completely. Spread the icing over the top of the cold cake, decorate with the walnut halves and serve.

tropical fruit salad

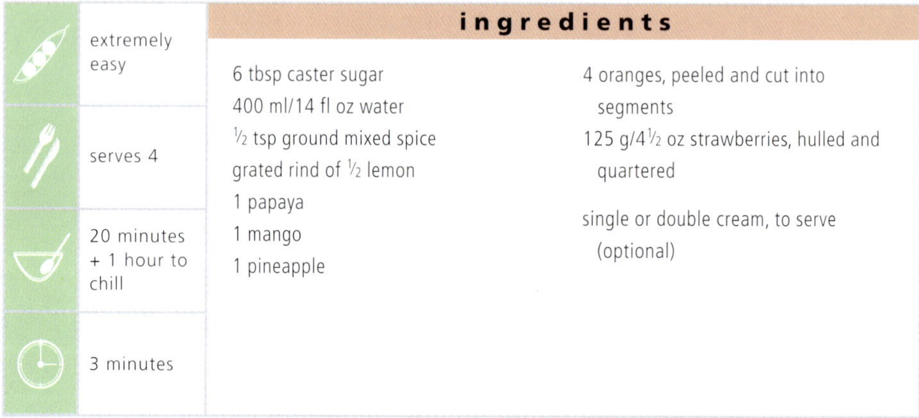

extremely easy

serves 4

20 minutes + 1 hour to chill

3 minutes

ingredients

- 6 tbsp caster sugar
- 400 ml/14 fl oz water
- ½ tsp ground mixed spice
- grated rind of ½ lemon
- 1 papaya
- 1 mango
- 1 pineapple
- 4 oranges, peeled and cut into segments
- 125 g/4½ oz strawberries, hulled and quartered

- single or double cream, to serve (optional)

Put the sugar, water, mixed spice, and lemon rind into a saucepan. Bring to the boil, stirring continuously, then continue to boil for 1 minute. Remove from the heat and leave to cool to room temperature. Transfer to a jug or bowl, cover with clingfilm and chill in the refrigerator for at least 1 hour.

Peel and halve the papaya and remove the seeds. Cut the flesh into small chunks or slices, and put into a large bowl. Cut the mango twice lengthways, close to the stone. Remove and discard the stone. Peel and cut the flesh into small chunks or slices, and add to the bowl. Cut off the top and bottom of the pineapple and remove the hard skin. Cut the pineapple in half lengthways, then into quarters, and remove the tough core. Cut the remaining flesh into small pieces and add to the bowl. Add the orange segments and strawberries. Pour over the chilled syrup, cover with clingfilm and chill until required. Serve with single or double cream, if using.

peach & strawberry meringue

easy	
serves 4	
30 minutes + 1 hour to cool	
3 hours	

ingredients

6 egg whites
pinch of cream of tartar
pinch of salt
275 g/9½ oz caster sugar
600 ml/1 pint double cream
250 g/9 oz strawberries, hulled and sliced
3 ripe peaches, sliced

sprigs of fresh mint, to decorate

Preheat the oven to 110°C/225°F/Gas Mark ¼. Line 2 baking sheets with baking paper, then draw a 25-cm/10-inch circle in the centre of each one. In a large bowl, whisk the egg whites into stiff peaks. Whisk in the cream of tartar and salt, then gradually whisk in 200 g/7 oz of the sugar. Continue whisking for 2 minutes until glossy. Fill a piping bag with the meringue mixture and pipe enough to fill each circle. Bake in the preheated oven for 3 hours. Remove from the oven and leave to cool completely.

In a large bowl, whip the cream with the remaining sugar. Put one meringue circle on to a serving plate, then spread over half the cream. Arrange half the sliced strawberries and peaches on the top, then top with the other meringue circle. Spread over the remaining cream, then top with the remaining fruit. Decorate with mint sprigs and serve.

chocolate cups

very easy

serves 4

30 minutes + 1¼–3¾ hours to cool/freeze

10 minutes

ingredients

6 egg yolks
150 g/5½ oz caster sugar
500 ml/18 fl oz milk
1 tsp vanilla extract
250 ml/9 fl oz double cream
1 tbsp grated lime rind
125 g/4½ oz organic dark chocolate, melted

thin strips of lime zest, to decorate

Beat together the egg yolks and sugar in a large heatproof bowl until creamy. Heat the milk, vanilla and cream in a saucepan over a low heat until simmering, then whisk into the egg mixture. Place the bowl over a saucepan of simmering water. Cook the mixture, stirring, until thick enough to coat the back of a spoon. Stir in the grated lime rind and leave to cool. Cover with clingfilm and refrigerate for 1 hour. Transfer to an ice-cream maker and process for 15 minutes. If you do not have an ice-cream maker, use the following freezer method. Put the mixture into a freezerproof container. Cover and freeze for 1 hour, then transfer to a bowl. Whisk to break up the ice crystals, then return to the container and freeze for 30 minutes. Repeat twice more, freezing for 30 minutes and whisking each time.

Invert a muffin tray and cover 4 mounds with clingfilm. Spread the melted chocolate over the mounds. Chill until set. Gently remove the clingfilm. Serve the ice cream in the cups, decorated with lime zest.

index